The Student's Guide to Successful Fundraising

How to Make a Plan, Make an Impact and Make Big Money for Your School, Club or Organization

Cara Filler

An Educateen Book

Published by

Cover design: Enrico Bobier

Edited by: Suzy Scullin

Dedication

This is for you. The powerful, dedicated, driven, unstoppable student who doesn't use excuses, like, "We don't have the money for that" or "We don't have the time to make that happen," to stop them from doing what's right, creating and funding amazing activities and leaving a positive lasting difference in their schools and communities.

You have laughed with me (sometimes at me), you have cried with me, and you have inspired me so much!

Thank you!

:: Table of Contents

INTRODUCTION

IF YOU'RE A student leader or educator on a mission to change the world, your school or your community, this is the book you've been waiting for. It's part guide, part idea book, part resource library – and it's all dedicated to helping you raise the funds you need to realize your goals and make a change.

Most fundraising books are loaded with suggestions like "recruit volunteers" and "ask for donations," but fall short of actually teaching you how to do that stuff.

This book is different. It's a **step-by-step guide** that walks you through the entire fundraising process. Instead of telling you what to do, this book actually shows you how to do it through simple steps, checklists, examples and templates.

By the time you're finished reading, you'll be a fundraising expert!

This book is split into three sections so you can quickly find what you're looking for, when you need it.

In Section One: Fundraising Fundamentals, you'll learn the steps that go into planning a fundraiser, plus get organizing tips like:

- How to generate an infectious buzz for your events
- Recruiting and organizing volunteers
- Perfecting "the ask" to get what you need from supporters
- Setting SMART goals for your group

Once you've mastered the basics, it's time to put them to good use.

Section Two: FUNdraising Ideas is filled with event ideas that raise spirits along with money and make a positive impact. You'll learn how to put your new skills to work, planning events like community-wide yard sales, service days and walk-a-thons.

In Section Three: Resources, you'll find everything you need to throw a successful event, including budget worksheets, sponsorship letter templates and sample pledge forms.

Put it all together, and you have a recipe for successful fundraisers that maximize your potential for outreach, education and plain old fun!

SECTION 1: FUNDRAISING FUNDA-MENTALS

Step 1—Find Your Mission

IT'S THE MILLION-dollar question: Why are you raising money? Is it to throw a rocking senior prom, finally get new uniforms for your team, support a charity or fund a class trip?

Whatever your need, clearly defining it is the first step toward achieving it.

Defining your needs helps you plan other aspects of a successful fundraiser, like a budget, and helps you communicate your goals to potential supports.

It's like asking your parents for money: Before Mom or Dad open their wallet, they want to know what you're going to do with the $20 inside. Potential donors will react the same way, and the first question they will ask when you approach them is "why?"

Your answer should be both specific and concise. A great mission statement answers both "what" and "why."

For example, the "what" may be new soccer uniforms, and the "why" may be because the old ones were designed in the 80s and are covered in grass stains, neon and tears. If your goal is replacing them, your mission statement might sound something like this: "We are raising funds to purchase new soccer uniforms to replace our outdated and worn ones."

Once you create a mission statement, practice saying it over and over again. It's the driving force behind your fundraising efforts, and you will be repeating it often to supporters, donors and volunteers.

It's time to put what you've just read into practice—it's time to take some action!

Take Action Now! Checklist

☐ **Create an awesome mission statement that answers the "what" and "why" of your fundraising needs.**

Step 2—Setting Fundraising Goals

NOW THAT YOU'VE defined your mission, it's time to set fundraising goals. People who set goals raise more money, and having clear benchmarks for success will help you define a budget and plan.

:: Setting SMART Goals

The fundraising goals you set should be specific, measurable, attainable, relevant and timely (SMART!).

Specific: Your goal should be well-defined and clear. Instead of saying "raising money for the band trip," it should include a concrete figure, like "raising $4,000 for the band trip."

Measurable: Your goal should be easy to measure and track. For fundraising goals, you may measure success in dollars.

Attainable: Unattainable goals don't motivate people to work harder; they just lead to frustration, which can quickly derail your efforts. Keep a forward momentum by setting goals that are attainable with the skills and resources you have.

Let's be honest – even the world's greatest bake sale is unlikely to pull in $10,000. But it may bring in $300, and that's a step toward your ultimate goal. Be realistic about your expectations, but remember that every little bit counts.

Relevant: Does your goal relate directly to your mission and cause? Does it match your needs and efforts? Is it worthwhile?

Timely: Setting a timeframe for your goal builds momentum and motivates both participants and donors.

Example of a not-so-SMART goal: "We want money for stuff."

Example of a SMART goal: "We will raise $10,000 to help buy eight new computers for the science lab by November 27."

See the difference??

:: Setting Individual Goals

Setting individual goals helps motivate group members and volunteers. To set individual goals, divide your total goal by the number of participants you expect.

For example: If your goal is to raise $10,000 for new computers and you have 30 participants, each individual should strive to raise about $333.

It's time to put what you've just read into practice—it's time to take some action!

Take Action Now! Checklist

- ☐ **Write down at least 3 SMART goals that will further your mission and cause.**
- ☐ **Set at least 3 individual SMART goals that will help motivate and guide group members and volunteers.**

Step 3—Make a Plan

YOU'RE NOW ARMED with a solid mission and goal. The next step is to outline your plan for reaching it!

The next section (*Section 2: FUNdraising Ideas*) is filled with fun, creative and proven fundraising ideas. Some will help you reach your goals better than others, but that's why we included a wide variety of suggestions.

There are four main types of fundraisers, and each has its benefits and pitfalls.

1. Event Fundraisers

Event fundraisers put the "fun" in fundraising and are great for building involvement and raising awareness about your group or cause. They may focus solely on fun or on providing a service, like a dance, walk-a-thon or car wash, and they take strong organization skills to pull off.

2. Collections Fundraisers

Collections fundraisers let you turn trash into cash. Your group may collect used ink cartridges, box tops or even soup labels and turn them into money through collections programs. If you take this route, do your research first because not all programs are created equally. The most lucrative programs often include incentives, like prizes or contests.

3. Passive or Partnership Fundraisers

Passive or partnership fundraisers generate donations when your supporters shop at certain stores or websites. Although these fundraisers require less work and investment, don't expect to break the bank without constant and strong promotion.

4. Product Sales Fundraisers

Product sales fundraisers, like selling holiday wrapping paper or cookie dough, are popular, but not all sales programs are the same.

Before you enroll in a product sales program, consider these factors:

- Product quality (Good or poor?)
- Product retail prices (Do the prices represent a fair value for customers?)
- Quality of the program's incentives or prizes
- Professionalism of company representatives

Ask these questions to learn more about the program:

- How long has the company been in business?
- What are the projected total profits to your school or group?
- What services are included in the cost of enrolling in the program? (indent and bullet list the following:)
- Order form tallying?
- Pre-packaging of products?

- Separation of individual orders?
- Freight and shipping?
- Presentations, videos or a kick-off assembly?
- Posters?
- Take-home packets?
- Product displays?
- Incentive or prize programs?
- Are product samples available?
- How are out-of-stock items handled? Are they substituted or back-ordered? How quickly?
- How quickly are damaged or incorrect shipments replaced?
- What are the payment terms?
- What is the return policy for products that are not sold?

Ask the company to provide references, and ask them the following questions:

- Did your group or school reach its goal?
- Did the company keep its promises?
- Would you work with this company again in the future?

It's time to put what you've just read into practice—it's time to take some action!

Take Action Now! Checklist

☐ **Decide which type of fundraiser will best help you reach your goals: an event, collection, product sales, or a partnership fundraiser?**

☐ **If you choose product sales, carefully research programs to choose the best one for your group.**

Step 4—Creating a Fundraising Budget

IT TAKES MONEY to raise money, and the earnings from your event must exceed the amount you spend on it, and hopefully by a lot. Creating a budget helps you set realistic goals, understand your limitations and determine the best type of fundraiser for your needs.

It's time to put on your thinking cap and imagine what your event looks like. Write down all the details you can think of, dividing them into two categories: income and expenses.

:: The Income Side

Estimate the money-raising potential of your event by talking to your core supporters, like parents, volunteers and other community members. You can also contact other organizations that have held similar events in the past to gauge your potential income.

The most successful fundraising events generate income in more ways than one. For example, a yard sale may also include a raffle and a bake sale, and a dinner event may be conducive to an auction.

Common income categories for fundraisers include:

- Food and beverage sales
- Individual ticket sales

- Sponsor donations (often in return for advertising)
- Table or group ticket sales
- Sponsorships of event participants (such as pledges)
- Sales of services or goods
- Advertising sales

:: The Expenses Side

This part of your budget includes everything you need to make your fundraiser a success. This is where your imagination really comes in handy – picture every aspect of your event and list all the details you can think of. After making your list, research quotes for each item to create a budget for your expenses.

Common expense categories for fundraisers include:

- Advertising and promotions (posters, flyers, invitations, postage, newspaper ads, web page development)
- Building/location/facility (space rental, tents, tables, chairs, set-up and clean-up costs, security personnel, site use permits)
- Production (sound and lighting equipment, technical labor)
- Food and beverages
- Decorations
- Insurance (may be required for certain events and venues)
- Miscellaneous (name tags, t-shirts, awards, prizes)

When in doubt, it's better to over-budget for expenses than to underestimate the cost of your event.

:: Calculating Profit

When you tally your final numbers, subtract the income total from your expense total. That number will be your expected profit for the event.

Your profits should be appropriate in relation to your expenses. For example, if an event costs you $1,000 to throw but only gives you a return profit of $200, you may want to consider a better way of spending your event budget. If it's a negative number, it's time to get back to the drawing board and find an idea that better fits your needs.

We've created helpful budget templates and samples just for you! To access them and create a solid budget for your fundraising event, check out *Section3: Resources* to find the download links.

It's time to put what you've just read into practice—it's time to take some action!

Take Action Now! Checklist

- ☐ **Use the sample budget template to guide you through the budgeting process.**

- ☐ **Calculate your fundraiser's potential income.**

- ☐ **Calculate your budget for expenses. Remember: it's better to overestimate than underestimate costs!**

- ☐ **Calculate your expected profits.**

- ☐ **Make sure your fundraising idea is profitable BEFORE moving on to the next steps!**

Step 5—Identifying Potential Supporters

GET OUT A pen and plenty of paper, because your list of potential supporters is going to be long. In fact, it's going to include practically everyone you know, plus some people you've never met before!

Who should be on the list?

Your mom, your Great Aunt Sally, your best friend, your friend's Great Aunt Susie, the postman, your former soccer coach, your neighbors, your hair stylist and nearly everyone else you know. If you limit your list to just friends and family, you limit your fundraising potential.

The next section of your list may include people you've never met before. They are local business owners, media personalities, community leaders and others that can help make your fundraising campaign a success.

Local civic organizations, like the Rotary Club or Kiwanis Club, can also be great fundraising resources. They may be able to connect you with even more individuals and organizations interested in supporting your cause, so add them to your list, too!

By now, your list should be pages and pages long, and that's great! All those names are potential supporters that can help you realize your goals.

It's time to put what you've just read into practice—it's time to take some action!

Take Action Now! Checklist

- ☐ **Make a list of potential supporters! Don't forget:**
  - **Family**
  - **Friends**
  - **Neighbors**
  - **Teachers and coaches**
  - **Community members**
  - **Local business owners**
  - **Media contacts**
  - **Community leaders**
  - **Local organizations**

Step 6—Reaching Out

ASK AND YOU shall receive...

If only it were that easy, right? Asking for donations can be scary, but with the right strategy and a little bit of practice, you'll be a fundraising pro in no time.

The key to asking for something, whether it's money, material goods or time, is to be authentic. Remember the mission you defined in the very first step? Always remember that it matters. Communicate that to your potential supporters in the right way, and you'll raise the funds you need.

Now, you can't just go walking up to someone and say, "Hey, can I have $50?"

If you take that route, brace yourself for dirty looks and getting yelled at. A lot.

Instead, follow these steps to perfect **"THE ASK"** and get what you need from your supporters:

1. Know what you're asking for:
Fully understand the mission of your group. For your supporters to believe in it, you have to believe in it yourself first.

2. Get small talk out of the way:
Start the conversation with the usual chit-chat: "How about

this weather, eh?" or "How's your mom doing?" This will break the ice and put you more at ease.

3. Make a transition:

After chatting for a few moments, make the transition to your fundraising efforts by saying "I want to talk about something important." This signals a change in the conversation to something more serious than the weather.

4. Make a connection:

Build a bridge between yourself and your organization by saying something like "As you know, I've been volunteering with..." or "I've been playing soccer for..."

5. Make them cry:

That may be going a bit too far, but your potential supporter should really understand why your mission is important and why you need their help. Tell a personal story about why your mission is meaningful to you.

6. Make the ask (gulp!):

Ask for something specific and concrete. Instead of just asking for $50, it's much more effective to say "Would you contribute $50 to pay for one uniform for our soccer team?" or "I'm trying to raise $500 for our school trip. Would you donate $50 to help me reach that goal?"

If you're asking for money, have a figure in mind and know what it will be used for. If you're asking for participation, talk about when and what role the person will play.

7. Say thank you:

Even if they say "no." You will sometimes hear "no," but that's ok. Refusals are part of the game. Don't let them discourage you.

Put it all together, and your conversation may sound something like this:

You: Hey Bob! How's it going?

Bob: Great, how are you?

You: Not too shabby. This weather is great, isn't it?

Bob: Yeah, it's a beautiful day!

You: The sun feels great! Listen, Bob, I'd like to talk to you about something important.

Bob: What's that?

You: Well, as you know, I've been playing the tuba in Riverdale's marching band for three years now. We've been invited to play at Disney World and it's a great opportunity for me as a young musician. I'd get to play alongside their own musicians and gain exposure for Riverdale. I'm trying to raise $1,000 for the trip. Would you donate $50 to help me reach that goal?

Bob: Sure thing sport! Who do I make the check out to?

You: Thank you so much, Bob! Your contribution will help me get to Disney World! I appreciate it so much and will send you a postcard while I am there!

What if Bob says no?

You: Thanks for considering it, Bob! I look forward to seeing you again when I come back!

You can also use the "ask" formula to ask Bob if he can volunteer at your next fundraising event or ask his own friends for donations.

That's it!

Practice it a few times in front of the mirror, with your friends, with your mom and on your mom's friends. The more you practice, the more natural it will become.

The spiel is pretty much the same whether you do it in person, over the phone, through email or by snail-mail.

If you're doing a written "ask," your proposal should be targeted, smart and focused. It should include:

- An introduction to yourself and your organization.
- A big-picture view of your mission and why it is impor-

tant.

- A clear "ask" that outlines what you specifically want to receive.
- A thank you!

You'll find a template for emails and letters in the resources section of this book. Use them as a basis for your fundraising letters, but don't forget to be authentic and let your personality shine.

:: What Are You Asking For?

There are three types of donations that can benefit your group: money, in-kind donations and time and services:

1. Money
It's great when people give you money. Every cent and dollar brings you closer to your goal, and you can budget monetary donations to meet your most pressing needs.

Donations of money can be used to benefit your cause directly or put towards fundraising events that can help you raise even more, but sometimes the most valuable donations aren't money at all, they are in-kind donations.

2. In-Kind Donations
In-kind donations are material donations. They might be anything from chairs and tables to sign-making supplies, dozens of chocolate chip cookies, tee-shirts, or even venues or

ad space.

Although your first instinct as a fundraiser may be to go after the big bucks, in-kind donations are often even more valuable than a check.

Local businesses and community members are often more willing to donate their goods or services than they are to write a check.

Soliciting in-kind donations increases your overall resources:

More resources:
Equals more power for your group to work effectively.

Cash is Uncomfortable:
Cash is a great resource, but some individuals and groups are not comfortable donating the green stuff. These same people will often be happy to donate other resources, and those resources can bring you closer to your goals if they match your needs.

Help Build Community Support:
In-kind donations also help build community support for your project. People who give in-kind donations become more connected to your cause. They want to see you succeed, and you gain new allies, good will and resources.

Fewer Strings Attached:
Material donations often come with fewer strings than cash.

Money from contributors can usually be spent in the way that best supports your project or organization, but some public funders limit the amount of their donation that can be spent on certain things, like renting a venue. In-kind donations carry no such strings, and you are free to use them to run the best program possible.

Access 'Cool' Stuff:

In-kind donations can also give you access to stuff you never would have otherwise. For example, a company may donate their old computers when they update their older machines. Instead of tossing them out, they give them to you. They provide a community service, and you benefit from getting something you wouldn't be able to afford otherwise.

Remember Expenses:

Remember the expenses side of your budget? You can cross many of those items off your list with in-kind donations, like food and beverages, venues, equipment and tables and chairs, therefore cutting the overall cost of your event.

3. Time and Services

This is another type of in-kind donation, and it may be the most valuable contribution you can get.

Volunteers donate their time and provide important services for your organization. They are the people who will sell tickets to your event to everyone they know, spend hours making promotional posters, show up early for the car wash with a smile and be the last ones to leave your dance-a-thon after boogying down all night!

In short, volunteers make your event dreams a reality.

In the next step, you'll learn ways to recruit volunteers and how to keep them happy.

It's time to put what you've just read into practice—it's time to take some action!

Take Action Now! Checklist

- ☐ **Review the awesome mission statement you created in Step 1.**
- ☐ **Decide which types of donations are most useful to your mission (money, in-kind donations or time and services).**
- ☐ **Create a written "Ask" using the template in the resources section.**
- ☐ **Practice "The Ask" on 3 friends or relatives.**

Step 7—Recruiting Volunteers

VOLUNTEERS ARE THE backbone of a successful event. They are the ones who arrive at the crack of dawn to set up tables, stay until the sun sets to help with clean up and manage crises of all sorts in between. They are the ticket-takers, the sign-makers, the car-washers and some of your greatest supporters.

Follow these tips to find them, make them an offer they can't refuse, use them wisely and treat them well:

:: Review Your List of Potential Supporters

Remember the list of supporters you made? Use it to find volunteers for your event!

:: Ask!

You already learned the most effective way to ask people for donations in the last step, so keep practicing by asking people to help out at your event. They can't help if you don't specifically ask them for it!

:: Be Flexible

Let's face it: No one really wants to spend their entire Saturday selling cupcakes at your bake sale. But plenty of people will gladly give up their morning or afternoon to staff the table, clean up crumbs and sell cookies. Instead of asking for a full-day commitment, break your event up into shifts if possible.

:: Tailor Your Opportunities

Everyone has a special skill or trait that can help your organization. Tap into what makes your volunteers special by pairing their skill sets and preferences with your needs. They will be more likely to offer their services, and you will benefit by getting their very best.

Trust your math-whiz friend with the cash box, hand a microphone to your classmate with the big personality and delegate sign-making duties to your pal whose notebooks are covered with doodles.

Create an opportunity for everyone who wants to help. If someone can't make your actual event, enlist his or her help beforehand.

If someone wants to volunteer for your dog wash but is allergic to fur, put them in charge of researching venues or following-up with donors. Never refuse an offer for help and create opportunities for everyone interested.

:: Communicate!

Volunteers cannot meet and exceed your expectations without first knowing what they are. Talk about the roles they will play before the big day to prevent them from running around like chickens with their heads cut off.

:: Bring a Friend

Ask every volunteer to bring a friend. You'll double your numbers instantly and gain more exposure for your group.

:: Everyone Loves Free Food

It's true! Offer snacks and drinks to your volunteers to keep them happy and energized throughout their shift.

:: Say Thank You

Volunteers are giving their time and energy to your cause for free. They deserve your gratitude, and you should show it with both a verbal "thank you!" and a sincere letter following your event.

You can even host a volunteer appreciation night at the end of each year to recognize the people who helped you reach your goals. You'll find a list of ways to say "Thank you!" to your volunteers in Step 9.

It's time to put what you've just read into practice—it's time to take some action!

Take Action Now! Checklist

- ☐ **Identify potential volunteers using your supporter list.**

- ☐ **Make a list of volunteer roles, and remember to be flexible and pair skills sets with your needs.**

- ☐ **Use "The Ask" to recruit volunteers for specific roles.**

- ☐ **Fill in volunteers on what you expect of them.**

- ☐ **Invite your volunteers to bring friends!**

- ☐ **Plan to provide snacks and drinks to fuel your volunteers during your event.**

- ☐ **Make a plan for saying "thank you" to your volunteers!**

Step 8—Create a Buzz

YOU HAVE A goal, you have donors, you have a plan, and you have volunteers—now you need supporters. It's time to promote, promote, promote!

School is a great place to start your promotion, but it shouldn't be the end point. If you want to raise big funds, you have to think bigger and reach out to your entire community and even surrounding communities.

People will support a worthwhile mission, but they have to know about it first.

Follow these tips to have everyone talking about your event:

:: Write a Press Release

The local media is always interested in what schools in the area are doing. Write a press release to grab their attention and get press exposure. Your release should paint a picture of your organization, goals and event, and it should include the following information:

- The name of your organization
- Why you are raising money
- Your goal
- How many people are involved

- Are community leaders or other civic organizations participating?
- What will you do at your fundraising event?
- Why is your mission important?
- What makes your organization special?
- Who will benefit from the funds raised and how?
- How can people help?
- When/where is the event?
- How much is a donation?
- Contact information

You'll find a handy dandy sample of a press release on the resources page .

:: Use Social Media

Remember when you changed your status on Facebook to "in a relationship" and the whole school seemed to know about it in .25 seconds!? Imagine getting that kind of fast, free publicity for your event.

Tweet about it, make it the subject of your status updates, post a teaser video to YouTube and snap Instagram shots of your venue or promo materials to build interest. If a picture of a cat can get re-tweeted 100 times in under a minute, so can the details of your event.

:: Build a Web Presence

These days, if something isn't happening online, it isn't happening. Get your event online by building a website that answers the 5Ws (Who, What, When, Where, Why?).

With services like Wordpress and Blogger, you don't have to know anything about coding to build an eye-catching website or compelling blog. Link your page to your social media sites and print it at the bottom of every flyer or poster to cross-market.

:: Old-School Strategies

Traditional promotion strategies are still effective for spreading the word throughout your school and community. Bust out your markers and poster board, write a story for the school newsletter, talk about your event on the daily announcements and put up flyers around your city and the surrounding areas.

It's time to put what you've just read into practice—it's time to take some action!

Take Action Now! Checklist

- ☐ Get exposure in local media about your event by writing an awesome press release. Use the sample in the resources section as a guide!

- ☐ Spread the word about your fundraiser on social media.

- ☐ Create a website for your event that answers the 5Ws, then cross-promote your event by linking it to your social media.

- ☐ Use old-school strategies like including your event in the daily school announcements, putting up flyers around your city and making posters to advertise your event.

Step 9—Say Thank You!

AFTER THROWING YOUR fabulous, fun event, thank the people that made it a success. You wouldn't be where you are now without them, so give great big 'thank yous' to your donors and volunteers.

You'll find a thank you letter template in Section 3, but remember to personalize it to make your donors feel as special as they are.

:: 10 Ways to Say THANK YOU to Donors and Volunteers

1. Host a volunteer appreciation night:
Supply snacks or throw a potluck, recognize the people who helped your fundraiser become a success, and celebrate your mission together.

2. Share progress with donors:
They love to receive updates and know that their donations are truly making a difference.

3. Create a video message:
Volunteers and donors will enjoy seeing your smiling faces and getting a personalized video message of thanks.

4. Send a postcard:
If you are fundraising for a trip, send your supporters a postcard to show you are thinking of them.

5. Acknowledge volunteers or donors:

Do this in your school or organization's next newsletter. Make sure they receive a copy!

6. Invite your donors to one of your group's activities:

This could include your next meeting, performance, rally or game.

7. Send photos of your group:

Ones of you in action work best. Send to donors and volunteers!

8. Whatever you do—make it personal:

Send a handwritten note, pick up the phone, send a group card with everyone's signatures and customize your message to the recipient.

9. Use your website and social media pages:

Use these resources to recognize and thank donors and volunteers in a public way.

10. Create customized certificates:

These are a great way to show thanks for the special people who most supported your cause.

It's time to put what you've just read into practice—it's time to take some action!

Take Action Now! Checklist

□   **Use the template in the resources section to create thank you letters for your volunteers and supporters.**

□   **Use one of the "10 Ways to Say Thank You" to celebrate the people who made your event a success!**

Step 10—Evaluate Your Event

THE CARS HAVE been washed, the cookies bought, the bands battled or the raffle won. Your event is over, and the first thing you should do is pat yourself on the back, high five your fellow group members and breathe a sigh of relief before you get back to work again.

Wait a minute —back to work again!?!?!?! I thought we were done...

Think again—you aren't done just yet. This tenth and final step will help you plan even more successful fundraisers in the future.

Before memories of your event details fade, get together with your group to talk about what worked and what didn't.

Go over your budget, comparing your estimated expenses and income with how much you actually spent and earned.

Talk through major stumbling blocks you encountered and brainstorm ways to avoid them in the future.

Admit your failures, celebrate your victories and write every-thing down so you can learn from your experience in the future.

Now, pat yourself on the back one more time—you did it and

you're closer than ever to your fundraising goals.

Remember what you learned and get on to the next mission!

It's time to put what you've just read into practice—it's time to take some action!

Take Action Now! Checklist

- ☐ **Make a list of what worked and what didn't at your event.**

- ☐ **Review your budget and compare it with how much you actually spent and earned.**

- ☐ **Talk about problems you encountered and plan ways to avoid them next time.**

- ☐ **Pat yourself on the back! YOU DID IT!**

- ☐ **Start brainstorming ideas for your next successful fundraising event!**

SECTION 2: FUNDRAISING IDEAS

NOW THAT YOU know the basics of hosting a successful fundraiser, put your skills to the test by bringing these FUNdraising ideas to life!

:: Walk-a-Thon

Fun, easy and healthy, this fundraising idea will bring you many steps closer to your goal. You can pull this off with as few as 10 people, but the more participants, the better.

The sooner you start planning this event, the more time participants will have to gather pledges, so get started early.

Step 1: Set a date, time and place for your walk-a-thon. Your route may stretch through your community, follow nature trails or simply loop around the school track.

Step 2: Create a pledge form for every participant based on distance or time walked. (You'll find a sample pledge form in the Resources section of this book).

Step 3: Secure individual pledges and collect larger donations from businesses.

Step 4: Promote your event! Post flyers around your community, advertise in the local paper and use social media to attract attention and crowds.

Step 5: The day of your event, provide water and snacks to walkers and have fun!

:: Variations

- Swim-a-thon: Collect pledges for laps or time in the pool.
- Bike-a-thon: Raise funds by pedaling for your cause!
- Dance-a-thon: Collect pledges for every hour of dancing and see who can last the longest on the dance floor.
- Stair Climbing: Take your fundraising efforts to new heights by climbing the stairs in a local office tower or landmark. Sponsors can pledge a few cents per stair to your cause.

:: Community Clean Up

- Lend a helping hand and clean up your community while raising money for your cause.
- Collect pledges for hours worked or the number of trash bags collected, or ask a local organization to sponsor your effort and pay for your time and services.
- Clean up a local park after a town celebration, hit the beach with trash bags and gloves or beautify another area of your community that needs it.

:: Variations

Provide the type of service your community needs most. It may be planting flowers in a neglected lot, painting a mural on an old building or raking leaves for elderly residents. Collect pledges to sponsor your service.

:: Holiday Gift Wrapping

The giving spirit is strong during the holidays! Crowds fill the malls and shoppers will be happy to make a donation to your cause in exchange for gift-wrapping services!

Step 1: Contact a local department store or mall and ask if you may set up a gift-wrapping station to collect donations and help during the holiday rush.

Step 2: Collect donations of supplies from businesses and community members.

Step 3: Don't forget to bring a jar for donations and information about your group to give to holiday shoppers!

:: Car Washes

With little planning and set-up, car washes are a fast and effective way to raise money for your group.

Step 1: Choose a venue for your car wash. Businesses are often willing to donate parking lot space for fundraisers. Look for an easily accessible and visible location on a main street where cars have room to line up for a wash. Gas station, grocery store and restaurant parking lots may be great options.

Step 2: Set a date at least a month in advance and recruit volunteers for time shifts. The more volunteers you have, the more cars you can wash and the more money you will raise!

Step 3: Ask for donations of supplies from local businesses and community members in return for advertising at your event.

You'll need:

- liquid soap
- brushes and sponges
- buckets
- hoses with spray nozzles
- lots of towels
- a cash box or bucket for donations
- signs

Step 4: Set a minimum donation price and sell advance tickets (plan for a rain date just in case!).

Step 5: The day of your car wash, send volunteers out to the street corners with signs while other volunteers direct traffic, collect donations and wash the cars. To move the process along, designate separate spaces for washing and drying.

Step 6: Supply sunscreen, snacks and water for your volunteers, play music and have fun!

:: Variations

Dog wash: If your volunteers are comfortable handling unfamiliar dogs, host a dog wash! Provide a shady area for waiting pooches and stock up on doggy treats for your clients.

:: Break the Dress Code

If your school has a dress code, this is a fun way to add variety while raising awareness and funds for your cause.

Step 1: Get permission from your school's administration to designate a special non-uniform day. Set a theme, like pajama day, crazy hats or ugly ties.

Step 2: Promote your fun day and collect contributions from students and faculty members who plan on participating. For $2, for example, students may get a special wristband or ticket that allows them to participate.

Step 3: Get decked out in your silliest gear and have fun.

:: Talent Show

Everyone has a hidden talent! Show off yours to raise money for your group.

Step 1: Choose a location, like your school's auditorium, set a date and recruit volunteers to be judges and work the event.

Step 2: Hold auditions, practices and a dress rehearsal. Recruit a stage manager and point person to handle details on the big day.

Step 3: Promote the show. Hang flyers, create social media pages and take out ad space in your local paper to spread the word.

Step 4: Sell advance tickets, charge admission at the door and sell concessions to boost your fundraising potential even more!

:: Variations

- Battle of the Bands: Rock out for a good cause!
- Art Show: Showcase student art by transforming your cafeteria or a community space into an art gallery.
- Comedy Show: Why was the tomato blushing? Because it saw salad dressing! Spend an evening trying to top that joke (it shouldn't be too hard).
- Poetry Slam: Turn a space in your school into a coffee shop for a night. Invite participants to share a favorite poem and sell cups of joe and snacks.
- Karaoke Night: Vie for trophies for best performance, most out-of-tune, best look-a-like, best singer and crazi-

est dance moves.

:: Face Painting

This is a great activity to add on to another event, like a carnival, sporting event or walk-a-thon. Transform faces into works of art (or lions, flowers or clowns) with some face paint, brushes and creativity.

Don't forget a mirror so your models can admire your work!

:: Variations

- Henna Hand Art: Henna is a plant-based dye that has its roots in India. Traditionally, it is applied to the hands or feet in intricate patterns.
- Temporary Tattoos: Scare parents throughout your community by offering airbrush or temporary tattoos that look real!

:: Coin Collection Ideas

Have you ever seen the amount of change hiding under your couch cushions? Go check yours right now. I'll wait...

Amazing isn't it!? Now imagine everyone in your school and community going through their own couches, purses, car floors and other hiding spots, taking all that change and donating it to your cause.

A school in Yellowknife, Canada, generates about $20,000 by doing this twice a year. You'll never look at a penny in the same way again! All those coins add up quickly.

:: Coin Harvest

Step 1: Decorate large jars with information about your cause.

Step 2: Place them around your school and throughout the community at businesses, libraries, entertainment venues, restaurants and other hot spots.

Step 3: Once a week, collect the change from each of the jars.

Step 4: Roll the change and cash it in at the bank.

Step 5: Be amazed how much money you've earned with so little effort.

:: Penny Wars

The goal of this spirited, friendly competition is for teams to collect as many pennies as possible while "sabotaging" other teams.

Coins are collected by each team in a clear container with a narrow neck, like a milk jug or large water jug. The containers are labeled with the teams' names.

Place the jars in places with adult supervision, like the library, homeroom or office.

Students donate pennies to their own containers. Teams earn one point for each penny placed in their own container.

Here is where it gets fun: Students attempt to "sabotage" other teams by placing quarters, nickels or dimes in their jars. Each of these coins subtracts points from that container. Quarters reduce the point total by 25, dimes cut it by 10, and nickels take away 5 points.

Containers can be counted daily or left to accumulate until the end of your fundraising period. Daily counting encourages friendly competition when totals are posted on blackboards, charts or whiteboards throughout your school. Keeping the counts a secret can encourage more speculative strategies and tactics.

The choice is yours, but either way, this is truly a FUNdraiser!

:: Raffles

You should have perfected your "ask" by now, so put it to use by getting in-kind donations you can raffle off to supporters, like gift certificates to spas or restaurants, jewelry, artwork, instruments, sports gear, travel packages and other goodies.

A raffle is a great complement to other events, like a walk-a-thon, dance or dinner. Hosting both events at once increases both your fundraising and fun potential.

Step 1: Solicit donations of raffle items from local businesses.

Step 2: Set a date and venue for your raffle.

Step 3: Advertise your event, highlighting special raffle items.

Step 4: Sell raffle tickets to everyone you know.

:: Variations

- Auction: Get a fast-talking volunteer to act as auctioneer and give away items to the supporters with the highest bids.
- 50/50 Raffle: Instead of going home with items, the winner gets half the ticket sales.
- Raffle off the chance to be principal or teacher for the day or spend a lunch or class period relaxing in a recliner watching movies.

:: Buzz-Off

This idea raises the fundraising stakes: Set a specific fundraising goal, and if you reach it before your deadline, a teacher, your principal or other person will shave their head in front of the whole school.

:: Jellybean Count

Lure people into donating to your organization with tasty jellybeans!

Step 1: Buy jellybeans (or another favorite candy, but stay away from chocolate or anything else that can melt), count them carefully and put them in a clear jar.

Step 2: Place the jar in a busy place, like your cafeteria or library.

Step 3: Charge people $1 to guess the amount of jellybeans in the jar.

Step 4: Record the guesses. At the end of your fundraising period, whoever guessed closest wins the jellybeans.

:: Orange Crush Sale

Got a secret crush? Let them know by sending them a can of Orange Crush.

Step 1: Buy lots and lots of Orange Crush.

Step 2: For $1, students can send a can to their crush.

Step 3: Deliver the cans, but remember to keep the names of the senders secret!

:: Variations

- Make students swoon by selling Valentine's day cards, candy grams or carnations

:: Movie Night

Host a night at the movies in your own school or ask a local theater for a portion of the ticket and concession profits for a night.

:: Eating Contest

There are few things funnier than seeing people dive into a pie head-first only to emerge with the dessert in their eyes, ears, hair and nose. If you have a taste for something other than pie, like hot dogs or ice cream, dig in! The concept is the same no matter what delicious treat you choose.

Step 1: Set a date and choose a venue.

Step 2: Get donations of your chosen food and prizes for the winner from local businesses.

Step 3: Advertise your event.

Step 4: Charge an entrance fee, sell tickets or have participants collect pledges for the number of pies or hot dogs they eat.

:: Snow Art Contest

Get everyone outdoors this winter by hosting a snow art contest.

Step 1: Set a date and choose a venue, like your school grounds or a local park.

Step 2: Contact local artists to participate in the event, and ask local businesses to donate prizes for the winners of the contest.

Step 3: Promote your event.

Step 4: On the day of the contest, charge spectators a small fee and sell hot chocolate to raise even more money.

:: Variation

- Pumpkin-carving contest: Celebrate Halloween and compete for bragging rights in categories like "Best Use of a Flaw," "Best Use of Power Tools," "Best Hair" and "Scariest Pumpkin."

:: Holiday Caroling

Belt out your favorite holiday songs throughout your neighborhood for donations. A beautiful singing voice is not required (but it will certainly help!).

Step 1: Organize small groups of carolers, set a route and pick a date.

Step 2: Print out information about your organization.

Step 3: As you sing door-to-door, hand out your info flyers and ask for a donation after spreading your holiday cheer.

:: Vegetable Market

If you have a community garden or many supporters with green thumbs, sell their fresh produce to raise money for your mission.

Step 1: Select a venue, like your school parking lot, and set a date.

Step 2: Ask your supporters for donations of fresh produce for your market sale.

Step 3: Advertise your market throughout your community.

Step 4: Sell items for 50 to 100% above the wholesale price.

:: Recipe Book

Convince your Grandma to share the recipe for her famous apple pie and collect favorite recipes from your group members and supporters.

Step 1: Create a book with the recipes you collect.

Step 2: Ask a local business to donate printing or copying services for your book.

Step 3: Create an order form for the book and sell copies at local events. Entice more people to buy by making samples of one of the best recipes.

:: Cash for a Bash

Have you ever just felt like smashing something? Channel that energy into raising money for your cause with this fundraising idea from SADD.org.

Step 1: Ask a wrecker to donate a car to your cause.

Step 2: Choose a venue, like your school's parking lot, and set a date (many students feel like hitting something around exam week).

Step 3: Advertise your event.

Step 4: Give participants pairs of safety goggles, and for a price, the opportunity to bash the car with a baseball bat.

:: Bowling Night

Strap on your bowling shoes and host a night at a local alley for your cause.

Step 1: Contact a local bowling alley and ask if they will donate a few lanes or a portion of profits for a night to your cause. You can also host a bowling competition with an entrance fee or a bowl-a-thon with pledges for participants.

Step 2: Advertise your event.

Step 3: Bowl your heart out and rack up funds for your group.

:: Variations

- Ask local restaurants, entertainment venues, sporting venues and other businesses to donate a portion of their profits for a day or night to your organization. You'll benefit from the donations while they benefit from the increased business your event generates.

:: Recycling Drive

Everyone has an old cell phone or ink toner lying around. Turn that trash into cash with a recycling drive.

Step 1: Collect old cell phones or ink toner cartridges from your supporters and set up donation boxes throughout your community.

Step 2: Sell them to a recycling program to earn funds for your group.

:: Community Yard Sale

People will be happy to clean out their garages, basements and attics for a good cause.

Step 1: Find a location, like a parking lot, large yard, field or driveway, and set a date for your event.

Step 2: Ask supporters to participate, and remind them to bring their own chairs and price their own items.

Step 3: Advertise your event in local newspapers, on social media and by placing flyers and posters around your community.

Step 4: Provide tables for sellers on the day of the event. Increase your profit by selling concessions at the sale or adding a raffle, and collect your earnings from each seller at the end of the day.

SECTION 3: RESOURCES

IN THIS SECTION, you'll find everything you need to support your fundraising plans, including worksheets, templates, samples you can download for free, from the downloads page, which you can access here: carafiller.com/sft/, plus a list of resources with even more fundraising ideas!

:: Downloads

Below is the full list of our helpful samples, checklists and templates! You can download them from here: http://carafiller.com/sft/

- Fundraising Event Budget: Expenses Worksheet

- Fundraising Event Budget: Income Worksheet

- Pledge Form Sample

- Donation Letter Template (in this book)

- Mail Donation Slip Sample

- Thank you letter Template (in this book)

- Donor Receipt Sample

- Press Release Sample (in this book)

- Fundraising Marketing Checklist (in this book)

:: TEMPLATES

ON THE next few pages you'll find some of the letter templates and samples included on the downloads page, in case you want to get started straight away!

:: Donation Letter Template

Date

Your Name
The Name of Your Organization
Your Street Address
Your Town/City, State/Province, Zip/Postal Code

Name of letter recipient
Title of recipient
Name of organization or business
Street Address
Town/City, State/Province, Zip/Postal Code

Dear Mr./Mrs. (recipient name):

My name is (your name) and I am writing on behalf of (your group name). Describe your group.

As members of (your group name), we strive to make a positive difference through our actions. We have started a project to (describe your mission, project goals and methods).

To reach our goals, we need (write down your request – and be specific!). We would be so grateful for your support and donation of these (funds/items) to help us achieve our goals.

Feel free to contact me at (your contact information) if you are able to help. Thank you for your consideration and I look forward to working with you to create a stronger community.

Sincerely,

(Sign your name)
(Type your name)
(Type your organization's name)

:: Thank You Letter Template

Date

Your Name
The Name of Your Organization
Your Street Address
Your Town/City, State/Province, Zip/Postal Code

Name of letter recipient
Title of recipient
Name of organization or business
Street Address
Town/City, State/Province, Zip/Postal Code

Dear Mr./Mrs. (recipient name):

On behalf of (your organization's name), I'd like to thank you for your generous donation of (amount of contribution, list of in-kind donations). Your contribution makes it possible for us to (state mission).

This year, our organization has (briefly describe goals achieved or growth). Contributions from people like you have made reaching those goals possible.

Once again, thank you for your generous donation.

Sincerely,

(Sign your name)
(Type your name)
(Type your organization's name)

:: Press Release Sample

Susie Scans
Riverdale High School
Phone: (123) 456-7890
Email: susiefundraiser@riverdale.edu
Riverdale.edu

Riverdale High School Students Launch Veggie Market Fundraiser

Riverdale, Indiana, April 27 –

Riverdale High School students are launching a vegetable market fundraiser to promote a healthy, environmentally-conscious lifestyle and raise $4,000 to purchase four new computers to replace the outdated ones in the science lab.

Students are partnering with the local Green Thumb Club to sell fresh produce every Saturday in May from 9am through 2pm in the high school parking lot. Green Thumb members will provide their own locally-grown fruits and vegetables, and the students will also be selling copies of their healthy Recipe Books based on some of the goods for sale. All proceeds from produce and book sales go directly toward purchasing new computers for the science lab.

For more information about the vegetable market fundraiser and how your support can make a difference for Riverdale students, please contact Susie Scans, fundraiser coordinator, at (123) 456-7890.

:: Fundraising Marketing Checklist

Use this checklist to guide your marketing efforts and keep track of tasks.

Fundraiser:
Dates of Marketing Campaign:
Marketing Leader:
Contact Information:

Newsletter or article write-up
- Writer:
- Proofreader/Editor:
- List of submission names and dates:
- Date of publication:

Press Release
- Writer:
- Proofreader/Editor:
- List of submission publications and dates:
- Date of publication:

Social Media
- Strategy and Content Leader:
- List of sites:
- Update schedule:

Organization Website/Blog

- Writer:
- Posting dates:
- Update manager:
- Update schedule:

Flyers and Posters

- Created By:
- Dates of distribution:
- Target Areas:

:: Additional Fundraising Resources

Check out these websites for even more fundraising ideas and advice!

Adopt a Classroom
This organization connects donors with classrooms so teachers have funds to purchase materials and resources.
http://www.adoptaclassroom.org/index.aspx

All American Card Company
Sell School Spirit Cards (discount cards) and make up to 90% profit.
http://schoolprogramfundraising.com/

The Association of Fund-Raising Distributors and Suppliers (AFRDS)
Information on product fundraising campaigns.
http://www.afrds.org/

Bammy's Gourmet Cookie Dough
Sell cookie dough to raise funds for your organization.
http://bammys.com/fundraising.html

Box Tops for Education
Collect box tops from hundreds of products to earn money for your club or cause.
http://www.boxtops4education.com/homepageinterstitial

Captain Planet Foundation

This group funds and supports environmental projects for students who want to create environmental solutions in their communities, homes and schools.
http://captainplanetfoundation.org/about/

Chuck E. Cheese's School Fundraising Program

Host an event at Chuck E. Cheese's and your group earns a percentage of all sign-up sales from food, merchandise and token deals.
http://chuckecheese.com/plan/fundraising/school-fundraiser

The Community Tool Box

Free info on essential skills for creating change and improvement.
http://ctb.ku.edu/en/dcfault.aspx

EdBacker

An online funding platform for educators.
https://edbacker.com/

ESPN Coaches Fundraising

Sell subscriptions to ESPN Magazine and your group keeps a percentage of the profits.
http://proxy.espn.go.com/coaches/index

The Foundation Center

Established in 1956, the Foundation Center provides a wealth of information about philanthropy, including an extensive

library of information on fundraising skills and identifying potential sponsors.
http://foundationcenter.org/gainknowledge/

The Fundraising Authority
Tools and information detailing every aspect of fundraising.
http://www.thefundraisingauthority.com/

The Funding Factory Fundraising Recycling Program
Earn cash and rewards for your organization by recycling electronics and ink cartridges.
http://www.fundingfactory.com/

Fundraiser Insight
Collection of fundraising ideas and articles.
http://www.fundraiserinsight.org/ideas/

The Fundraising Plan
Fundraising ideas and inspiration.
http://www.believekids.com/blog/

Fundsnet Services
A resource database about philanthropy, fundraising and grants.
http://www.fundsnetservices.com/

Green Schools Initiative
A collection of green fundraising tips to raise money with minimal environmental impact.
http://www.greenschools,net/section.php?id=47

Healthy School Fundraiser Ideas

Ideas and advice on hosting healthy school fundraisers from the Association of State and Territorial Public Health Nutrition Directors.

http://www.astphnd.org/resource_files/233/233_resource_-file5.pdf

http://www.astphnd.org/resource_files/233/233_resource_-file6.pdf

IdealWare

Advice on evaluating and choosing online donation tools.

http://www.idealware.org/articles/few-good-online-dona-tions-tools

Kids Gardening

Connects students with grant money to fund gardening programs that increase learning, environmental awareness and health.

http://grants.kidsgardening.org/

Labels for Education

Collect caps and UPCs from thousands of products to earn merchandise for your school.

http://www.labelsforeducation.com/

The Learning Center Network for Good

Free online fundraising resources for nonprofits.

http://www.fundraising123.org/

Minnesota Council on Foundations
An excellent overview of grant proposal writing.
http://www.mcf.org/system/article_resources/0000/0325/writingagrantproposal.pdf

OneCause
Through OneCause, supporters can give to your organization by shopping online with hundreds of well-known merchants. Supports save money on their purchases and your organization gets a portion of the profits.
http://www.onecause.com/

Popcorn Palace
Sell snacks for your organization and keep 50% of the profits on each item.
http://www.popcornpalace.com/Home/Fundraising

PTO Today's Fundraising Page
Information on fundraising strategies and planning from the Parent Teacher Organization.
http://www.ptotoday.com/fundraising-strategies

Restaurant.com Fundraising Gift Card Program
Sell gift cards for over 18,000 locations and keep up to $10 per card sold.
http://incentives.restaurant.com/landing-pages/fundraising

School-Fundraisers
Offers an array of sales fundraising programs, including flower bulbs, nuts and snacks, jewelry, cookie dough and more. Pro-

grams require no money upfront, and groups can earn up to 50% profits on their sales.

http://www.school-fundraisers.com/

SchoolMate Fundraising

Sell cookbooks and keep 50% of the profits. Program includes free promotional posters, and all items are pre-sold.

http://www.schoolmate.com/other-products/fundraising/

SchoolSpirit Coffee

Sell specialty coffee with customized labels to raise funds and keep 50% of the profits.

http://www.schoolspiritcoffee.com/index.html

Target's REDcard Program

When your supporters shop at Target using a REDcard, your school gets 1% of their purchases.

https://www-secure.target.com/redcard/tcoe/home

Tupperware Fundraising for Schools

Sell Tupperware products and keep 40% of the profits.

http://worldwideplastic.com/tupperwarefundraising/tupper-ware-fundraiser-schools.html

FINAL WORD

:: What's Next?

Now that you've gotten to the end of this book, you should have a clear understanding of what you need to do to make a fundraising event successful and make BIG money for your school, club or organization.

This book will be constantly updated and there are plans to produce a second version with even more ideas in the future.

If you'd like to be notified about when the paperback version comes out, please send an email to info@carafiller.com and I'll add you to the notification list!

If you have any questions or feedback, I'd welcome an email from you! You can get me at info@carafiller.com

:: About the Author

Cara Filler is a youth motivational speaker, prevention specialist, author and entrepreneur with a passion for helping people realize their full potential. For nearly 20 years, Cara has spread her message about the power of choice to audiences around the globe, and her life-changing story has made her one of the most sought-after and admired female inspirational speakers in the field.

Cara's mission was sparked by the tragic death of her identical twin sister, Mairin, the day after their 18th birthday. This unimaginable loss became the driving force behind Cara's powerful campaign of changing attitudes and saving lives.

From that day forward, Cara committed to helping others put life and its challenges into perspective. With honesty, passion and oodles of humor, she delivers an inspirational message that has captivated and changed audiences across the world.

Cara is also the founder of the Drive to Save Lives tour, a hand-picked group of high-impact, high-quality prevention speakers, and iSPOKE UP, a campaign for students to share their voice, speak up for others and make positive choices.

When Cara is not speaking, writing or changing the world, she enjoys spending time at home in Vancouver, Washington, with her husband, Jason, their adorable son, Jaxson, and their playful dog Sadie.

If you'd like to get in touch with Cara, here are her details:

- Email: info@carafiller.com
- Web: www.carafiller.com and www.drivetosavelives.com
- Facebook: www.facebook.com/drivetosavelives
- Twitter: www.twitter.com/carafiller

:: Can you help?

If you liked this book and it was helpful to you, could you PLEASE leave a review on Amazon?

Reviews are really important to the success of a book—so if you like (or don't like!) what you've read, PLEASE take 2 minutes to leave your honest review—I really appreciate it.

Thanks, Cara